IT JOBs
Be Your Own Guru

Chitralekha

"What You Should Know"

DEDICATION

Never lose faith in life...

God never leaves our side...

Trust in him and bad times will slide...

Dedicated to all my family and friends.

With your love and grace, I have reached here.

Contents

Preface

This book deals with prototyping the IT management life that is the initial stages of making choices and going through selection process of a career in the IT World, plus how you can evolve and grow in your career with all latest information, tips and tricks and fixes in self grooming required for you to launch ahead in this world as a mega prosperous release. You can be an IT Guru on your own. We have reached a time in our lives, where every information is crucial, and the more we get, the less it feels to keep ahead in this changing world. Right knowledge at right time is very important and guidance really helps. This book also provides tips and tricks on how to manage your work and various template examples which can be used to create documents for work purpose. This book provides a valuable window on dealing with various aspects of work culture in an IT world and how to deal with them. This book is a must have for all IT career aspirants. All the Best!

Thanks & Regards,

Chitralekha

From Simple dreams to IT dream

On a beautiful starry night, I dreamt of becoming a Scientist ten years back, but lesser did I knew I would land up head over heels in the IT World…. From Biology Labs to IT companies, the journey has not been straightforward.

I was a simple student, mediocre at first, and when I jumped to college I started suddenly gaining higher scores and topping class. I really did surprise myself. In-fact I did my graduation in Zoology,

Botany & Chemistry with good grades and I topped in Chemistry in my batch. I was proud of my achievement, but I was not aware, I will not be using them anywhere in my career ahead. I then enrolled for my post-graduation in Biotechnology and got out with flying marks and honors too. Teachers were proud of me, and I wanted to become a Doctor or Scientist desperately. In all past years with graduation and post-graduation I kept attempting medical exams and I even got through some exams, but could not get a seat due to heavy donation some colleges asked for. Well it was a pity. I had worked in research institutes also in my vacations and holidays and attained special merit certificates, not to forget them but neither were good enough to get me a job in Science field, as that required further research work or Ph.D. Then suddenly one day, I landed into the IT dream.

I heard my friend applying for a BPO organization exam, where in if you get selected, you will get a job and good salary and you will also get to learn IT domain work and grow a career for yourself. I jumped for it and cleared the exam and interview. Then began my journey into the unknown. From a science background I took a 180 degree turn into IT

sector. Oh! what a leap,

I still remember the day of getting my first job

offer letter in my hand, and it was so valuable to me. I

dreamt of a settled life, and freedom from learning,

and also a big fat salary, but dreams are dreams.

Graduating students these days dream of working in

Private IT companies with good brand name, and

earn a good reputation, name and fame for them....

well is it so...what first comes in mind is good salary

package and what is the reality today, we do not have

a pay structure suitable for all salary types and so the

dreams are only dreams. We complete are graduation, and then post-graduation these days, as it seems mandatory and basic requirement, then dream of the world lying down at our feet which will fulfill all our wishes as soon as we land in one IT organization. We even believe that IT Organizations need us and are waiting to immediately hire eligible talented people like us. Well reality is quite different and will shake you to core.

Nobody guides or provides exact scenario and situations that are there in real world, not even in college or in all books. It's like, when you are children you dream of Prince, Princess, Unicorns and castles which are unrealistic and when you just step adulthood, you land into dreams of a successful job, a robust career and home and good salary. Well ideally there should be a special class in college to make you ready for outer world, to prepare you for milestones in life ahead. That is very much necessary these days.

Challenges of Modern IT World

IT industry work going on anywhere is a Business, and do not make a mistake to take it otherwise. All idea of any perfect IT person or any perfect IT organization is only a dream and a personal satisfaction thought. People working and doing their daily tasks rarely realize that they are part of a huge market competition. They just see competition amongst colleagues and strive to excel. IT work like all other business is just buying and selling and management of same with IT assets and infra.

Any IT organization, anywhere in the world, will have many challenges, like doing continuous improvements and stay ahead of others with Technology and retain talented people in their organization. Also, inventing something new, like a new process or a new idea for team building, and even new automations are ongoing tasks which are important. All challenges change over time, and new certifications keep coming for people to learn, making stabilization in one position difficult if you are not moving along the flow.

With so much technology and population everywhere, everything you can think of is going up, like inflation, data consumption, money spent, and even prices for everything around us, but what is going down is profit margin. Investors these days want more profit in less spend. Organizations try to

provide best customer service, do all hard work day

and night and still what matters in the end is whether

customer really got satisfied or not for what was

delivered. Even a small appreciation matters a lot to

us for all our hard work, in fact that motivates us to

work more.

What is more challenging is changing jobs now,

as jobs are less, roles are varied and not defined

anywhere or standards are not set, even if you get all

types of certification, every organization has their

own way to judge a person is right or not for their

position. You can give myriad interviews, crack exams but still wait for that golden chance to land up in your lap. On every job portal too there are millions of jobs listed, but when you keep trying you feel, people cannot see what exactly is your talent and domain expertise. Reskilling and upskilling is the demand of the hour. You have to keep yourself updated to gain promotion and even move to another role in same organization or outside, Automations are causing more domains to vanish and are increasing job loss.

Organizational structures everywhere are also not aligned to employee benefits and satisfaction, you can keep following up with HR for Internal Job postings or some queries, but getting a satisfactory response is very rare and time taking task. Requests are sometimes even ignored and or denied by HR and Managers, as suitable to company policies. Many companies do not support with higher education or certification or training required for work to be done.

Marketing of all products correctly and in time, is very important. Same as keeping ourselves up to date with technologies coming in. Now is the time for

Cloud and as everything is moving on cloud, privacy and security are major concerns with sales of any product or services. Data protection and privacy rules are mandatory now for everyone to know.

With outsourcing in multinational companies, offices are around the globe and challenges are to manage work and people, with cultural difference, language barriers and time zone changes. People applying for Visa and waiting for it to be approved are endless. Processes are not easy or demands time, money and too many forms to be filled. With increasing technology advances, you are asked to work online and use video meetings instead of travelling to client to save money and visa processing hurdles.

Around the globe practices being followed are not end to end useful and standard, in spite of dozens of Standards available to settle them. Every organization has leverage of tailoring their templates, and processes, and hence causing more confusion, so to do same work in two departments, you might have to learn the whole work again.

Companies these days if are providing incentives and bonus then you are lucky, as soon it will be bygone. Annual increments are not enough to meet inflation rate. In fact, people everywhere are being laid off and there is target of 10 to 30% every quarter.

Leadership challenges are in every organization and departments where what you are doing at base level, may not go up to higher managements and somebody else might get all appreciations. Governance models are not robust and strong everywhere. There is lack of proper communication from top to bottom. Growth of data and money spent every year in maintenance and procurements and salaries are increasing but nothing is benefited to employees even if company shows growth in their profits every quarter.

In today's generation what matters is show that you and only you are doing all the work, rest is to be left behind, do smart work with hard work. So we have to change, learn and leap and be strong, Are you ready for changes? Career guidance helps in gaining skills and knowledge and it is important at high school level.

Demystify Information Technology & Information Security

IT is part of Information Systems. The four

components of an information system are --

- Information technology

- Process

- People

- Structure

- Efficiency

IT or Information technology as defined by Wikipedia is the use of computers to store, retrieve, transmit, and manipulate data, or information, often in the context of a business or other enterprise. Network, Storage and Computing are the three main elements of IT.

IT is considered to be a subset of information and communications technology. Or we can say that Information technology *is* the broad subject concerned with all aspects of managing *and* processing information, especially within a large organization or company. Hence, an information technology technician is a computer support person who can work for various companies. They should have an associate's degree, bachelor's degree, or certificate in a computer field. IT technicians may look into obtaining certifications to promote job potentiality.

Parts of IT or its components are Hardware, Software, Database, Telecom and Human Resources. All have to be learnt about and managed for a successful career. Being well educated in terms and processes in all above will help you with every kind of work and project in the IT arena. Hardware can be from Laptop, Desktops, Server to Routers and Network Switches, Access Point controllers and peripherals that are used in offices like Keyboards and Mouse. Software can be from Windows operating system or MAC OS, to applications and other IT tool software used by industry specific people for their daily work. Telecom devices includes Ethernet cables, fiber optics, desk phones, softphones etc. While Human resource will focus on team members and management of hiring of same. A senior IT manager needs to also see how well he can get work done from all people available in his team in a timely fashion. Database or Storage box is important for storing data and regular backup of all data to prevent loss of same, is crucial. Databases and data warehouses have assumed even greater importance in information systems with the emergence of Big Data, a term for the truly massive amounts of data that can be collected and analyzed. Learning and training of employees also is required and to track data of all work done to see what all happened in past so that same mistakes can be avoided in future, or we do not have to reinvent the wheel. All our work related applications are now completely automated, thanks to the IT sector. IT professionals are people involved in essential management of sensitive data, exclusive computer networking and systems-engineering. The advancement of the IT sector has resulted in automation of all systems in use with Admin or IT teams, and even for users for business as usual work for daily operations. It has also led to production and use of data and made data available to all for use with security. More communication and business has grown everywhere because of IT, which has helped with streamlining of business processes. IT has also helped in timely upgrade of all hardware and software and maintenance of same too. Global social gathering on devices has grown and online presence everywhere has let to faster communication and deals and also making loved ones feel safe in family while traveling. Network has made the world a shorter place now but we have grown dependent on these IT stuff and systems. Not to mention how IT also helps in data collation, research work and analysis and investigation for medical research, drug creation, surgical procedures and even helps world armies with data of maps and navigation systems globally.

From entertainment to fashion industry, and from education to government, all are dependent on IT now. Hence IT management is one of the most beneficial careers these days.

Most people understand that global economic infrastructure is becoming increasingly dependent upon information technology, and no information system is 100% secure. Information security is one of the topics that everyone knows of, but most are not really aware of the finer details. Many computer users simply think that their firewall and antivirus software provide them with all the protection they need to keep their computers secure. However, as mischievous hackers become more resourceful, and users add more and more information into a growing number of databases, there exists an increased exposure to hacker attacks, information surveillance, and other security breaches. Information systems, operated by governments and commercial organizations are vulnerable to attacks and exploitation through their Internet connections. Workstations connected to the Internet are currently the most common targets of malicious hackers. As a result, information assurance is a very serious concern for individuals, businesses, and governments.

Not only do we need to be aware of how attacks are

executed, but we also need to learn how the systems

can be protected against different attacks.

Hence, not only is IT important but IS that is

Information Security is equally important in IT world.

Knowledge of both will help you to succeed as they

go hand in hand with every step of work. Malware is

a software that is specifically designed to disrupt,

damage, or gain unauthorized access to a computer

system. Information security and knowledge of all

types of malware, can help you understand how to protect your systems better.

In the past decade, two developments have brought information security management issues to the fore. First has been the increased dependence of organizations on information and communication technologies, not only for key operational purposes but also for gaining deliberate advantage. Second, supported by information and communication technologies, the whole business model for many organizations has been transformed. Whereas in the past companies could rely on limiting themselves to a particular geographical area to conduct their business. Today companies are increasingly becoming location self-governing and are finding themselves to be strategically deprived if they are confined to a particular place. The importance of advances in information technologies and the changing limitations of the firm have brought the importance of data and information to the fore. This is because it is information that helps companies realize their objectives and helps managers to take adequate decisions. In the business model of the past, data and information to a large extend was confined to a particular location and it was relatively easy to protect it from falling in the hands of those who should not have it. Because information was usually processed in a central location, it was also possible to ensure, with a relative degree of certainty, that it's content and form did not change and ensure that it was readily accessible to authorized personnel. In fact, maintaining confidentiality, integrity and availability were the main tenants for managing security. Today because the nature of the organization and scope of information processing has evolved, managing information security is not just restricted to maintaining confidentiality, integrity and availability.

IT infrastructure management is equally important, from looking into all hardware like Server, Storage, Switches, and also on Software and Solutions, you can conquer most demanding workloads of a project. Working on Business continuity plan and disaster recovery for a company is also crucial to take care of all hardware and resources in case of a natural calamity. Managing an IT department poses unique challenges including staffing, budget management, project management and leadership.

Learn IT management skills, strategies, and tips from leading IT experts by reading about them and their work and how they have managed their companies so well.

Is IT Career your Passion

Now when you understand what IT is, think over for a good career decision, is IT really your career choice and your passion. Then it is a good choice. Hold your thoughts, take a dep breath and move on.

You are going to embark a journey where you will feel satisfied and get to learn a lot too. Things you love to do, if you make it your career, then it doesn't feel like a burden or an extra work, it is fun. Now to make your IT work passion a success, following some discipline in life is required wherein you also believe in IT world, learn IT terms to speak and follow standardized documents for your everyday work.

IT Job designation may be as follows depending on your work and company policy too, just to name a few --

- IT Manager/ Deputy IT Manager/Senior IT Manager

- Project Manager

- Program Manager

- Solution Architect

- Software Developer

- Scrum Master

- Data analyst

- Network Engineer

- Network Administrator

- Security Specialist

- Computer Scientist

- Data Scientist

- Cybersecurity Engineer

- Systems Analyst

- Business Analyst

- Cloud Engineer

- DevOps Engineer

- Automation Engineer

- Tech Support

- IT Consultant

- AI /Machine Learning Engineer

- Software Tester

- Service Desk Engineer

It is important that we understand the enigma of salary. Salary is personal to everyone and should never be disclosed, and in an IT organization you have to follow the guidelines laid done by the HR for same. How your salary package is designed depends on your luck, company policy, company pay structure, eligibility to particular pay grade or band in the company and on your past experience to showcase the same. Now every organization and every team in it has its own pay differences even in one particular team, so for example, all people in IT team in a company will not get same salary. Also,

don't expect everyone to be open and or transparent

in office with all policy and process details. You need

to do your homework on your own, and maybe

search all policy sites and keep yourself updated.

People working in a group sometimes tend to hide

things, and even some managers, but what will make

you a good manager is to be open to all and be

transparent.

When you become an IT Manager always keep

in mind the following points that will help you – Be

accommodating, keep learning, listen to your

colleagues and staff and take up new certifications to increase your technical knowledge.

Get Organized & Make Plans

To survive with daily IT management work, one should focus on making plans ahead of time and tracking all activities. Being organized is the soul mantra for IT life. Breathing life in and out of hectic timelines and stressful targets can lead to health issues. Hence make sure that you standardize all types of documents and templates and create a work plan or strategy to focus on target or goal and timeline.

Cost assessment is also very crucial and saving money here and there will lead you to benefits. Risk management is another crucial aspect of IT management. One should forecast activities and cost and should be able to see risks associated with all steps. Then best way to mitigate them is to sit with all teams and stakeholders and take out solutions and or look for mitigations and contingencies. Following a schedule every day with a dedicated checklist will help you work through huge tasks with simplicity.

Learning never ends

However old you get, always remember learning never ends. Time is money and it is essential not to waste any single moment and learn and grow. Train yourself from basics to master level of all education and certifications that are required in your area of work. Google is the best friend and You tube best teacher these days. Make use of them, devise a list of all to do certifications and degrees and go for it. With all upcoming latest technologies, you will have to keep yourself up to date with details of the future.

If you stop learning, you will become like that stagnant pond of water that does not have any chance to flow or grow and meet the river. You must keep self-learning targets every year and dedicatedly finish them. This way you would be a content and happy person, not only personally but also socially you will have more knowledge and topics to interact in. Time management for learning is a crucial aspect as it if for personal life too.

Gain as much work experience as possible, as that will help you see what all is going on in the world of IT and open your eyes to new learning and new avenues too. Work experience will also lead to more respect and more salary in society.

Cross-training and skill development in various domains is very important these days. For example – Not only should you be able to understand how a server works but also see how it can be connected and made on by a network engineer. Hence to build a server for example and make a site ready with new servers, you need to check on hardware, network and security parameters.

Be curious and Keep learning. Expand your mind.

Basic Education required in Reality

With the blink of an eye, there is a change in the real world. There is no standard for basic education in reality, all or whatever you do, you have to do any ways, and it is then also not enough. Every year course and matter changes and even level of basic education that really matters also changes per decade. Earlier being graduate was deemed so prestigious, but now If you don't have a master's degree, nothing matters. Doing Master's is just the base cake, on top of that several other Degree course toppings and certification icings are important to make life fruitful and meaningful for various jobs in market. Every field has their own basic certification also that is basic to them like in IT industry, for its management of process and general working, ITIL course is important, similarly in the field of Internal Audits, Certified Internal Auditor certification is important. Every person wanting to grow in their career path has a new learning specific to them. To keep up to the market standards that is to face competition and increase self-worth also, learning new technologies and frameworks are important every year. If you do not invest your time and money on them, you will lag behind.

Work hard in silence, let your Success make the noise.

Icing on the Top: Certifications to do

The world of Certifications is vast, In IT

industry too it depends you are in which specific domain and hence myriad certification options for growth are available. Certifications not only help you gain education in quick time but also enhances your skills in Resume and to your management in any company. What certification is suitable to you depends on which line of work or area of work you are getting into, what do you want to do in future and will that be helpful in your career path. A certification is a credential that you earn to show that you have specific skills or knowledge. They are usually tied to an occupation, technology, or industry.

Certifications are usually offered by a professional organization or a company that specializes in a particular field or technology. In any or every exam these days, you have to solve multiple choice questions and or go through real world or IT world work scenarios and answer questions from them.

The certifications provided by the biggest certifications providers, are, just to name a few --

- Microsoft (Microsoft Certified IT Professional, MCSA/MCSE, Microsoft Certified Technology Specialist, etc.)

- ITIL 4

- ISFS

- CompTIA (CompTIA A+, CTP+, CDIA+, Network+, etc.)

- Cisco (CCNA, CCDA, CCNA Security)

- CISSP: Certified Information Systems Security Professional

- CISM: Certified Information Security Manager

- CompTIA Security

- CEH: Certified Ethical Hacker

- GSEC: SANS GIAC Security Essentials

- Adobe Certifications

- TOGAF 9

- Prince 2

- AWS Certifications

- Microsoft Certifications

- Oracle Certifications

- PMI Certifications/PMP

- VMware Certifications

- Risk Management

Whatever certification you choose, make sure you do enough research work first and see if it fits your career plans and is apt for your abilities. Get training on it and go for exam then. You can find all material and details about all certifications on Google and you can work on them accordingly. To confirm your ability to show to others that you can use and work on a specific technology doing certifications are a must for any IT job. There is a sea of knowledge from which you can choose which area or domain to go to but that also keeps changing every day, with evolving technologies. Certifications do not guarantee you a good job bit definitely put your resume on top of the pile.

Certifications will give you advantage over others and

also showcase your skills to the world. It is a must in this rapid changing world and will help you in more and better career options. You can even ask for promotion or higher salary if your company management agree to it. Sales team can show your credentials to new clients to gain new opportunities for your company.

Reach out to the Clouds

Cloud computing is the major driver in leading business processes and growth these days. It is the use of hardware and software to deliver a service over a network. With cloud computing, users can access files and use applications from any device that can access the Internet. Cloud computing is basically computing over internet including storage, application and servers. Data processing through provision of scalable information and infrastructure on various platforms in a leading technology intervention of today. Cloud Computing is of below types, depending on what you choose or require as a service base to be for your work --

- IaaS (Infrastructure-as-a-Service)

- PaaS (Platform-as-a-Service)

- SaaS (Software-as-a-Service)

Cloud based software tools and private data centers will rule in future. Cloud knowledge and certifications have become a must have these days, as the world is revolving around Cloud services and facilities in every IT company. AWS, Azure and Salesforce are top 3 Cloud computing Companies providing basic to advanced level certifications which can be easily done. Also a lot of matter is available on their community pages, blogs, Google articles and YouTube, including demos. Characteristics of cloud computing are as follows which helps in all types of

work and will lead the way in future --

- On-demand self-service

- Broad network access

- Multi-tenancy and resource pooling

- Rapid elasticity and scalability

- Measured service with cost

- Easily deployable models

- Simplified IT Management & Maintenance

- Built-in Security

- Remote Access

- Cost Efficient

- Reliable Delivery, Management, and Support

Service

Be the Search Engine

Keep yourself updated with data, news, and

process knowledge, that will always help. Not only

news but IT knowledge and details and news about IT

companies, IT products, process and lifecycle of and

how all activities are done, are all crucial aspects of

one's journey into an IT Career. How this helps is like,

if anyone anywhere has any query any time, it would

be good to answer them, that will not only showcase your knowledge to others but would also make you famous and popular with colleagues and managers. This can also help you with your appraisal and taking up new roles for growth or movement in other departments of your choice. Also people who are experts in not one but at least more than one domains or areas are generally given preference over all in appraisals and travel etc. for projects too.

Increasing memory by doing brain exercises of solving puzzles and or playing detective games always helps. When your brain has a habit of learning, that really helps, as you can consume more data and process it in brain. Also, revising activities and steps frequently and reading a lot of books will sharpen your memory and help you stay one step ahead than others. Hence reading books about IT, and IT products and processes will also help, but apart from that reading all other general books or even fiction helps in increasing your awareness and skills. Why is it so important to be at a level where you know and understand all in latest technology news and updates is because in this competitive world with so much population if you are not progressing and growing along with new developments you will lose

and somebody else will get the chance you deserved.

Keeping abreast with all technology changes and why

they were done, were there any risks and what are

cost changes with all new features is a must these

days, because then only you will be able to suggest for

a suitable solution to your customers as per their

need.

"Be The Expert everyone wants to see...."

Use Templates of every kind for more professional work

Templates are very important for daily BAU work and also for all kinds of data collection, preservation and dashboard reporting etc. Templates can be made for all kind of work being done and can be easily saved and reused as required. Templates can be easily made by yourself, and basic needs of a good template is as follows –

- Serial Number

- What this template is about, summary or topic and points

- What is cause of work

- What is required to be done

- Who will do it

- What can be Risks

- What will be mitigation plan

- What will be timings or schedule for that work

- What will be backup plan

- Comments, status or updates for work done to track its progress.

Once you create a template, you can always add rows or columns to give it more meaningful shape and matter as required. Template are easy way to show progress, track updates and can be updated daily, weekly or monthly as per requirements. You can also make dashboards out of it to show meaningful analysis and graphs of same data that is captured. Templates can be made in a Word or Excel file and data can be presented to clients on a MS power point slide with summary and graphs.

These days you have online free templates available for MS PowerPoint presentations and excel reports to be made on varied forms, flowcharts, timelines, milestones, patterns, and with graphs and diagrams to help you make your work easy. They can be downloaded from websites and used directly. Their features, topics, content and color all can be modified or customized as per requirements. Also Google has slides and templates built in as Google Slides which can be leveraged. You can also create master sheet and databases on Microsoft SharePoint to use for continuous updates, trackers and even to showcase as

Dashboards.

Never stop doing your best, just because someone

doesn't give you credit.

Time Management & Work Life Balance in IT

I feel, time is a relative state of moving space

which leads to entropy of all things. It is there but it is

not there still for us to see it, though we all are

undergoing it and ageing. Hence, to achieve a lot in a

short lifespan, we need to learn Time management. If

we do not focus on ourselves and our work right now, then nobody else would. We are owners of our own life and how we manage time is completely on us. If we are working for 9 hours in a company, then the other 9 should be for our family and us.

Start your day with always making a plan for the day itself, keeping in mind all priority tasks that needs to be done. If required do make a note of it somewhere, or keep a diary or excel sheet where you can plan your work in time. Do divide all important activities in durations suitable and try and finish the then exactly in same time. Keep marking all activities as closed once you do it. This will give you a sense of achievement also when all tasks are completed. Cross-check all that was required to be done and then speak to all stakeholders or teams to check if anything is left. Maintain a project tracker or plan and or Kanban board to track backlog and come back on it to keep regular checks in place.

Being stress free is very important. Don't let daily IT work stress you out, whatever work has to happen, if you have planned it, and going in correct direction towards target, will ultimately get done. So as mentioned earlier also, you should keep track of your work, that will help in timely focus on points which are crucial for activities or something that you might miss out. There can be excel sheets where you can track your daily or weekly project progress, or business as usual operations activities to be taken care of. Also, revise or go through your sent mails daily, for at least couple of days old mails, so that you can check, if anything is not done yet.

Maintaining a work life balance is much required, hence take care of yourself and your family first, then you will be able to work much better. Health should always be first priority in life. Exercise, do meditation, drink lots of water and whenever you feel angry, just try to relax yourself. Remember anger is not good and doesn't lead you to your promotion. Hence if required do deep breathing at that time to relax. As much oxygen reached your body, it will help all organs inside. Eating healthy and getting a good night sleep are equally important for a fresh day start. Be in nature as much as possible and take out time for yourself and your hobbies too in life, nurture love around you. Rely on and trust your friends and family as they will support you. Satisfaction also comes from giving, and hence donate food and money to the needy if possible.

Work Life balance can be achieved if you pay attention to your family members and take care of them so that they never feel left out. At the same time, try to keep all work related activities to be done at office only, so that it doesn't stresses you out or others in your family. Time management hence is crucial here. Apart from work, it is also important that you delve into brain development activities and games or puzzles. Even reading books is best for brain. Physical activities and sports are important too to keep you active and fit, plus divert your attention to something that you can enjoy and also increase your concentration. Music on the other hand is a soother and also teaches patience if you learn to play one musical instrument yourself. These things help in life for a complete self-development.

Don't keep huge expectation. Huge expectations in any field of life is not fruitful, and always leads to sadness if not met. Similar with IT industry work life, if you expect huge salary increase, and repeated appreciations, or growth and career development every now and then or every year also, that is not possible and does not happen anywhere for everyone.

Expectations are our thoughts which remain with us in back of our mind and keep pushing us to work and be hopeful and strive hard, they are our dreams too in a way, but they should not be made rigid in our mind. Expectations should always be there to push you higher towards more hard work and disciplined life to achieve success.

Live in reality, but be hopeful. Nothing Worth Having Comes Easy!!!

In fact, be grounded and grateful always, that is the way to lead your life.

Future of IT

IT jobs and Information technology itself will survive in coming years because there is ongoing research and development and need of continuous change in IT gadgets, systems and processes. Adapt to changes and you will survive, that should be your goal, and hence it is rightly said that only change is constant in life. Traditional or old customs, processes, systems or tools cannot be used ten years down the line, hence we need to evolve with increasing data and knowledge. Few arenas like Cloud Computing,

Medical data management, AI, Machine Learning and Block chain IT will empower society with inventions and technologies that will lead to a powerful future.

Medicine domain data management is the biggest technology change coming up. In fact, Health information technology is the application of information processing involving both computer hardware and software that deals with the storage, retrieval, sharing, and use of health care information, data, and knowledge for communication and decision making improve the quality of healthcare while reducing costs; improve the coordination of care and information among hospitals, labs, physicians and other healthcare organizations; ensure that personal health records remain secure; and. promote the early detection, prevention and management of chronic illness. healthcare domain data management. Health IT improves the quality of healthcare delivery, increases patient safety, decreases medical errors, and strengthens the interaction between patients and healthcare providers. automation in data management for genetics data.

Artificial Intelligence simulation technology are helping with vehicles for safer driving and for agriculture, education and aviation etc. Artificial refers to something which is made by human or non-natural thing and Intelligence means ability to understand or think. Machine learning is the scientific study of algorithms and statistical models that computer systems use to perform a specific task without using explicit instructions, relying on patterns and inference instead. It is seen as a subset of artificial intelligence. For Machine Learning Algorithms, you will need to understand subjects such as gradient decent, convex optimization, quadratic programming, partial differential equations and alike. It helps computer to learn all data and can even predict or find out repetitive behavior and help with analysis without human intervention. Automation in IT, Robotics & Internet of Things (IOT), Big Data, 3D Printing, Virtual Reality, Block chain, Digital Wallets are all latest technologies spreading fast across the globe. Automation helps in increasing productivity rates while also helps with better use of materials and saves time. Block chain technology can be used to create a permanent, public, transparent ledger system for compiling data on sales, tracking digital use and payments to content creators, such as wireless users or musicians. Block chain is being used in healthcare, IT, asset management and application management. Also, IOT is stealing the show these days with ways to generate real-time data that we can analyze and use to create desired business outcomes.

All above will be used massively in Healthcare, Manufacturing plant, Government, Education, Retail, Food Industry, Hospitality, Financial services, Professional services, Technological companies and even in Non-profit organizations. IT has been solving problems for human society in every way and will continue to do so. So if you are thinking of moving

into IT management career, go ahead and make a

start.

All the Best!

About Author

Chitralekha

Chitra is an India based IT Process Consultant, Service Management & Project management expert. She was born and brought up in North India. She also has work experience in IT delivery, BAU operation management, Strategy and Portfolio development and Process Documentation & Consultation.

She brings in quality in her work with in depth ITIL Service Management knowledge of managing IT industry & departments, with exposure & experience in Incident, Change, Problem handling and Audits. She has been with many IT companies since 2005 and has managed many Accounts in varied roles earlier. She is Double post-graduate in Biotechnology and Operations Management with Honors. She is ITIL MALC Expert and IRCA Lead Auditor with Prince 2 Foundation & Practitioner certification. She is also Exin Certified Integrator in Secure Cloud Services. With her positive attitude, Operations & Project management skills she will surely go a long way in creating success.

She is an active speaker and people motivator. Her goal in life is to touch people's heart so that they can to do good to others and be kind. She loves travelling around the world and is also an efficient Tarot Reader and Diviner. She believes in helping others and caring. She is grateful to her parents and family for all love and support.

She is recognized with Professional Awards in various organizations for her performance and outstanding work. She was also recognized as Quality Champion and Process trainer. She has won Hamdard Scholarship for high rank in Biotechnology and Maulana Ali Mian Scholarship for academic brilliance, and Margaret Wallace Best Science Student Scholarship in her study days.

She is reachable at unifiedconscience@gmail.com

"The Mystery of Life

is not a Problem to be solved,

but a reality to be experienced.

Believe in God."

* 9 7 8 1 6 9 3 8 0 7 7 1 8 *